The Miracle of Life: A Week-by-Week Guide to Fetal Development

Preface

In this book, we will explore the fascinating journey that a baby undergoes during its development in the womb. From the first weeks of pregnancy to the exciting day when the baby finally comes into the world, we go through each week and describe the important events that take place. To make it easier to follow, we will divide the book into three trimesters and review the most significant stages of development week by week. We hope you find this book both informative and rewarding as you learn about this amazing process.

The Miracle of Life: A Week-by-Week Guide to Fetal Development

Introduction to pregnancy and fetal development

In this chapter, we will provide an overview of the phases of pregnancy and the most important stages of fetal development. We will explain how pregnancy is divided into three trimesters and how fetal development goes through different stages from conception to birth.

1.1. The stages of pregnancy

Pregnancy is divided into three trimesters, each lasting approximately 13 weeks. The three trimesters mark different stages in the development of the fetus and the bodily changes of the mother.

- First trimester (weeks 1-13): Fertilization, implantation and the early development of the embryo take place during this stage. It is also during this period that most of the fetus's organs are formed.

- Second trimester (weeks 14-26): During the second trimester, the fetus begins to grow faster and the mother can feel its movements. The organs continue to mature and the fetus develops its nervous system, hearing and vision.

- Third trimester (weeks 27-40): During the last trimester, the fetus continues to grow and prepares for birth. The mother's body also undergoes changes to prepare for childbirth.

1.2. Stages of fetal development

Fetal development can be divided into several stages, from conception to birth. Here is an overview of the main steps:

- Fertilization: The sperm and egg fuse to form a zygote.

- Implantation: The zygote attaches itself to the uterine wall and forms an embryo.

- Embryogenesis: During this period, organs and body structures are formed.

- Fetal period: After the eighth week, the developed embryo is called a fetus. During this period, the organs continue to develop and mature, and the fetus grows in size and weight.

- Preparation for birth: During the last weeks of pregnancy, both the fetus and the mother's body prepare for childbirth. The fetus begins to position itself head down, and the mother's body undergoes changes to facilitate birth.

It is important to remember that every pregnancy is unique, and fetal development can vary slightly from week to week. The information in this book is intended to provide a general overview of what to expect during pregnancy, but individual differences may occur. If you have any questions or concerns about your pregnancy, it is recommended that you consult a doctor or midwife.

In the next chapter, we will begin to go through each week of pregnancy, focusing on the most important events and changes that occur in fetal development. We hope this detailed review gives you a deeper understanding of the fascinating process that takes place during these nine months and strengthens the special bond between you and your baby.

First trimester: Weeks 1-13

In this chapter, we will dive deep into the first trimester of pregnancy, which spans from week 1 to week 13. We will follow this amazing journey week by week, and in addition to detailing the development of the embryo, we will also advise on what the mother can do to optimize the conditions for her child's health and well-being.

2.1. Week 1-2: The spark of life and a healthy start

When the sperm and egg meet and fuse to form a zygote, the spark of life is created. The zygote undergoes an amazing journey as it moves through the fallopian tube and divides many times to become a blastocyst. Implantation occurs around day 6-10 after fertilization, when the blastocyst lovingly attaches itself to the uterine wall and develops into an embryo.

To give the embryo the best start in life, the mother should maintain a healthy lifestyle and eat a balanced diet rich in folic acid, iron and calcium. Taking a prenatal folic acid supplement is especially important during this time, as it can help prevent certain types of birth defects in the brain and spine.

2.2. Week 3: A symphony of cells and the importance of nutrition

During week 3, the embryo's early development begins, where three cell layers are formed: ectoderm, mesoderm and endoderm. These layers will give rise to a variety of organs and body structures, paving the way for the complex symphony of life. A small heart and blood vessels also begin to form, which is the first step in the creation of the circuit that will bring oxygen and nutrients to all cells in the body.

To support this process, it is important for the mother to get enough nutrients. Continue to eat a nutritious diet and take your prenatal supplements. Avoid raw or undercooked foods, which can contain harmful bacteria, and limit caffeine and alcohol intake.

2.3. Week 4: First heartbeat and rest

At week 4, the embryo's heart begins to beat and pump blood, which is one of the most fascinating and moving aspects of early fetal development. The nervous system and spine also begin to develop, laying the foundation for all communication and coordination within the body.

During this time, the mother may begin to feel tired and may experience nausea. It is important to listen to your body and rest when needed. Continue to eat small, nutritious meals throughout the day and drink enough water to stay hydrated.

2.4. Week 5: A kaleidoscope of organs and exercise

During week 5, the development of the embryo takes a big step forward. A kaleidoscope of organs begins to form, including the lungs, liver, pancreas and kidneys. The brain, which is the center for thoughts, feelings and experiences, is divided into five different parts. Eyes and ears also begin to develop, preparing the embryo to meet and experience the world that awaits outside the womb.

To support this development, the mother should continue to eat a nutritious diet and consider adding more omega-3 fatty acids, which can promote brain and eye development. Light exercise, such as walking or swimming, can also be good for the mother's health and well-being.

2.5. Week 6: A face takes shape and dealing with nausea

At week 6, the embryo's face begins to form and becomes more recognizable. Eyes, nose and mouth become more clear, and even the first outlines of arms and legs begin to appear. It is a very exciting time in the development of the embryo.

The mother may experience increased nausea during this time. It can be helpful to eat small, frequent meals and to have a few crackers or a piece of bread by your bed to eat before you get up in the morning. Avoid strongly spiced and fatty foods and try to eat foods with more neutral flavors.

2.6. Week 7: Development of the skeleton

During week 7, the fetal skeleton begins to develop from cartilage to bone, including the skull, spine and limbs. This is an important milestone in fetal development as it prepares to face a world of movement and activity. Nerves and muscles begin to work together, making the first small movements possible. The mother should continue to eat a nutritious diet that includes calcium to promote a strong skeletal structure and support the growing musculature of the fetus.

2.7. Week 8: Continued organ development

During week 8, the fetal organs continue to develop and mature. The heart divides into four chambers and begins to pump blood more efficiently. Liver, kidneys and other internal organs are also forming and preparing to perform their important functions. At this time, the fetus' ears and nostrils begin to form, and the head develops rapidly. The mother should continue to eat a balanced diet and take her prenatal supplements to support this critical phase of development.

2.8. Week 9: Movements and gender differentiation

At week 9, the fetus begins to make its first movements, although the mother cannot yet feel them. These movements are a combination of spontaneous twitches and more goal-directed movements in response to stimuli. Sexual differentiation also begins during this time, and the external genitalia begin to form, although it is still too early to determine the sex of the fetus. It is important for the mother to continue to take care of her own health and eat a nutritious diet to support the continued development of the fetus.

2.9. Week 10: Fingers and toes

During week 10, the fetus's fingers and toes become clear, and the small joints begin to form. This is an exciting time as the fetus prepares to grasp and touch the world around it. The skin is still very thin and transparent, and the blood vessels are clearly visible under the skin. By this time, the fetus has also developed basic facial structure, with eyelids covering the eyes and a distinct upper and lower lip. The mother should continue to eat a nutritious diet and take her prenatal supplements to support this critical phase of development.

2.10. Week 11: Proportions of the head

At week 11, the fetus's head begins to get more proportional sizes in relation to the body. The brain continues to grow rapidly, developing complex neural structures responsible for both conscious and unconscious functions. The fetus's face also develops, with the nose and ears becoming more pronounced. At this time, the fetus can swallow and also suck on the thumb, which is an important preparation for life outside the womb.

The mother should continue to eat a nutritious diet and drink enough water to support the continued growth and development of the fetus. It is also important to avoid exposure to harmful substances, such as tobacco smoke and alcohol, as these can have negative effects on fetal development.

2.11. Week 12: Muscle coordination

During week 12, the fetus's muscle coordination begins to improve, which means that the movements become more controlled and goal-oriented. The fetus can now stretch and bend its limbs, and the first reflexes begin to develop, such as the grasping reflex. The intestines, which were previously part of the umbilical cord, now move into the fetal abdominal cavity.

The mother should continue to eat a nutritious diet, rich in vitamins and minerals, to promote the muscle and nerve development of the fetus. It is also important that the mother continues light physical activity to support her own well-being and maintain a healthy pregnancy.

2.12. Week 13: End of the first trimester

At week 13, the first trimester ends, and the risk of miscarriage decreases significantly. The fetus has developed from a zygote into a complex, proportionate and active being. The fetal organs and systems have formed and will continue to develop and mature throughout the rest of the pregnancy. At this time, the fetal genitalia have also developed to the point where the sex can be determined by ultrasound.

The mother may begin to feel more energetic and less nauseous during this time. It is important to continue to eat a nutritious diet and take your prenatal supplements to support the continued growth and development of the fetus. Continue to communicate with your healthcare provider about any questions or concerns that may arise during pregnancy.

Second trimester:

Weeks 14-27

During the second trimester, fetal growth and development continue to accelerate. The mother may experience a reduction in nausea and fatigue and begin to feel fetal movements. In this chapter, we will explore the second trimester week by week and offer advice on how the mother can continue to support her baby's health and well-being.

Week 14: A new phase and improved energy

As the second trimester begins, the mother may feel an improvement in her general well-being. Fetal organs and structures continue to develop and mature. Hairs and fine hairs, called lanugo hairs, begin to grow on the body of the fetus. It can be a good time for the mother to plan for parental leave and start preparing the home for the new family member.

Week 15-16: Fetal movements and mother's adaptations

During weeks 15 and 16, fetal movements become more noticeable, which is an exciting milestone in pregnancy. The mother may need to adapt her wardrobe to accommodate the growing belly. Continue to eat a nutritious diet and consider adding extra fiber to prevent constipation. Fetal skin is still very thin and transparent, but pigment begins to develop, and eyebrows and eyelashes form.

Weeks 17-20: Anatomy ultrasound and fetal sex determination

Between weeks 17 and 20, most mothers undergo an anatomy ultrasound, where the fetal organs and structures are carefully examined. It may also be possible to determine the sex of the fetus at this time. The mother should continue to follow a healthy lifestyle and talk to her healthcare provider about any questions or concerns. The fetal heart now beats with a more regular rhythm, and the skeleton continues to strengthen and mineralize.

Week 21-24: Bonding and mental health

During weeks 21 to 24, the fetus begins to react more to sound and touch. It is a good time for the mother to start creating an emotional connection with her baby by talking, singing or playing music to it. The fetus also begins to practice breathing by drawing amniotic fluid into and out of the lungs. The mother should pay attention to her own mental health and seek support from family, friends or professionals if necessary.

3.1. Week 14: Hair, eyebrows and eyelashes

In week 14 of pregnancy, hair, eyebrows and eyelashes begin to form on the body of the fetus. This week is full of exciting changes that help give the fetus more human features and prepare it for life outside the womb.

To begin with, the hair follicles on the fetus's head develop, and fine hairs begin to grow. These hairs are very thin and soft, and they will continue to grow and thicken over the coming weeks. In addition, lanugo hair is formed all over the body. Lanugo hairs are thin, fine hairs that protect and insulate the fetus in the womb. These hairs will fall out before or shortly after birth, but they play an important role in the development of the fetus during this time.

Eyebrows and eyelashes also begin to form during week 14. These small details give the fetus more pronounced facial features and help protect the eyes from debris and light as they develop. The eyes are already quite developed at this point and continue to mature. Although the fetus's eyelids are still sealed, they will open and begin to function later in pregnancy.

The fetus's facial muscles also develop during this week, allowing it to make different facial expressions, such as grimacing and frowning. Although these movements are involuntary at this point, it is an important part of fetal neuromuscular development.

During week 14, the mother may feel increased energy and should continue to eat a nutritious diet to support fetal growth and development. It is also important that she continues to take her prenatal supplements, such as folic acid and iron, to reduce the risk of complications during pregnancy. The mother should also consider increasing her intake of zinc and biotin, as these nutrients are important for hair growth and can help support fetal hair, eyebrow and eyelash development.

Following a healthy lifestyle and eating a nutritious diet during pregnancy is essential to support fetal development and well-being. By giving the body the nutrients it needs, the mother can help her child develop and grow in the best possible way during this exciting time in life.

3.2. Week 15: The skin and bones

During week 15 of pregnancy, the fetus's skin and bones continue to develop and mature, which helps give it a stronger and more proportionate body shape. This week marks further progress in the growth and development of the fetus, preparing it for life outside the womb.

The fetus's skin becomes thicker and more transparent during week 15. The skin consists of several layers, and the outermost layer, called the epidermis, begins to form a protective barrier against infection and damage. In addition, a layer of fat develops under the skin, called subcutaneous fat, which helps to insulate and protect the fetus. In the coming weeks, the skin will continue to develop and become less transparent, but at this point it is still possible to see the fetal blood vessels through the skin.

The bones continue to strengthen and the length of the bones increases during week 15, giving the fetus a more proportional body shape. The bones and cartilage begin to remodel into harder bone structures, and the bone marrow begins to produce red blood cells. The fetal skeleton also becomes more visible on ultrasound at this time.

The mother should make sure she gets enough calcium and vitamin D to support fetal bone development. Calcium is important for building strong bones and teeth, while vitamin D helps the body absorb calcium. Eating foods rich in these nutrients, such as dairy products, dark green leafy vegetables and fish, can help ensure that both mother and fetus receive the necessary building blocks for strong bones.

During this week, the mother should also continue to eat a nutritious diet and take her prenatal supplements, such as folic acid and iron, to reduce the risk of complications during pregnancy. It is also important that the mother begins to prepare the home and plan for parental leave, as the baby's arrival approaches.

Week 15 is an exciting time in pregnancy, as the growth and development of the fetus continues to progress. By eating a balanced diet and taking care of her health, the mother can help her child develop and grow in the best possible way during this important time in life.

3.3. Week 16: Taste buds and hearing

Week 16 of pregnancy means further progress in the development of the fetus's senses. During this week, taste buds and hearing begin to develop and improve, giving the fetus the opportunity to experience new tastes and sounds from its surroundings.

Taste buds develop on the fetus's tongue and palate during week 16, and it begins to sense flavors from the mother's diet through the amniotic fluid. The amniotic fluid, which surrounds and protects the fetus, changes taste based on what the mother eats. This early exposure to flavors can influence the child's food preferences later in life. It is therefore important that the mother eats a varied and nutritious diet during pregnancy, to give the fetus a variety of tastes to experience and get used to.

The fetus's hearing also improves during week 16. The small bones in the middle ear and the nerve cells in the inner ear continue to develop and mature, allowing the fetus to hear sounds from both inside and outside the womb. This includes the mother's heartbeat, the rumbling of the stomach and even the mother's voice. It is a good idea for the mother to start talking and singing to the fetus, as it can hear her voice and will recognize it after birth.

To ensure healthy development of the fetus's taste buds and hearing, the mother should continue to eat a nutritious diet and avoid strong flavors that may adversely affect the fetus. She should also avoid high sound levels and exposure to noise, as this can affect the fetus' hearing development.

The mother should continue to take her prenatal supplements, such as folic acid and iron, to reduce the risk of complications during pregnancy. Maintaining a healthy lifestyle and eating a balanced diet is essential to support fetal development and well-being throughout pregnancy.

Week 16 is an exciting time in pregnancy, as the development of the fetus's senses takes great strides forward. By giving the body the nutrients it needs, the mother can help her baby develop and grow in the best possible way during this important time in life.

3.4. Week 17: The kidneys and bladder

During week 17 of pregnancy, the internal organs of the fetus continue to develop and mature, with particular focus on the kidneys and bladder. This week is crucial for the fetus's ability to produce and excrete urine, which is an important part of its growth and development.

The kidneys, which are responsible for filtering and purifying the blood and producing urine, begin to function during week 17. The fetus begins to produce urine which is secreted into the amniotic fluid. This urine production and excretion is an important part of fetal development, as it helps maintain the balance of fluids and electrolytes in the fetal body and helps create a stable environment for growth.

The urinary bladder, which stores urine before it is excreted, also develops during this time. Along with the kidneys, the bladder plays an important role in maintaining the body's fluid balance and eliminating waste products.

To support fetal kidney and bladder development, the mother should continue to eat a nutritious diet and drink enough water. It is important for the mother to get enough fluid, as it helps maintain a healthy amniotic environment for the fetus. She should also continue to take her prenatal supplements, such as folic acid and iron, to reduce the risk of complications during pregnancy.

In week 17, the mother should pay attention to the movements of the fetus. While it's normal not to feel fetal movement regularly at this point, it may be a good idea to start noting when the fetus is active and discuss any concerns with your doctor or midwife.

Week 17 is an important time in the development of the fetus, as the kidneys and bladder begin to function and contribute to creating a stable and healthy environment for the growth of the fetus. By eating a balanced diet, drinking enough water and taking care of her health, the mother can help her baby develop and grow in the best possible way during this critical time in life.

3.5. Week 18: Movements become more visible

During week 18 of pregnancy, fetal movements become more visible and noticeable to the mother. The fetus's muscles have developed enough that it can now perform more complex movements, and the mother can feel these movements as "kicking" or "bumping." These movements are not only an exciting milestone for the parents, but also an important indication that the development of the fetus is progressing as it should.

The movements of the fetus at week 18 mean that it can stretch and bend its limbs, twist its body and even hiccups. These movements are an important part of the motor development of the fetus and help it develop muscle strength and coordination. The mother can also begin to feel the rhythmic movements of the fetus when it hiccups, which is a normal and healthy part of fetal development.

To support fetal motor development and movement, the mother should continue to eat a nutritious diet and take her prenatal supplements. It is also important that the mother continues to exercise regularly and maintain a healthy lifestyle, as this can contribute to a healthy pregnancy and support fetal growth.

The mother can also benefit from tracking fetal movements, especially as she approaches the third trimester. By noting when and how often the fetus moves, the mother can be aware of any changes in fetal activity and discuss any concerns with her doctor or midwife.

Week 18 is an exciting time in pregnancy, as fetal movements become more noticeable and give parents a stronger sense of connection with their growing baby. By eating a balanced diet, exercising and taking care of her health, the mother can help her child develop and grow in the best possible way during this important time in life.

3.6. Week 19: Genital development

During week 19 of pregnancy, the genital development of the fetus continues. At this time, the external genitalia begin to become more distinct, which may allow the parents to discover the gender of the fetus through an ultrasound scan, although this is not guaranteed.

For male fetuses, the testicles mature and begin to produce testosterone, which is important for the continued development of the male genitalia. In female fetuses, the ovaries continue to develop and already contain millions of egg cells at this time.

In addition to the development of the genitals, the growth and maturation of the fetus continues in week 19. The skin is still thin and transparent, but the subcutaneous fat begins to form, giving the fetus more fullness and roundness. The limbs of the fetus continue to grow and the proportions begin to resemble those of a newborn child more and more.

To support fetal genital development and overall growth, it is important that the mother eats a nutritious diet and takes her prenatal vitamins. It is also important that the mother avoids harmful substances, such as alcohol, tobacco and certain medicines, as these can adversely affect the development of the fetus.

The mother should also continue to move and exercise regularly, as long as it is safe and comfortable for her. Exercise can contribute to a healthy pregnancy and help the mother manage weight gain and other pregnancy-related ailments.

Week 19 is an important time in the development of the fetus, when the genitals continue to mature and the fetus grows and develops rapidly. By eating a balanced diet, taking care of her health and avoiding harmful substances, the mother can help her child develop and grow in the best possible way during this critical time in life.

3.7. Week 20: Sleep cycles and kicks

During week 20 of pregnancy, the fetus begins to develop more regular sleep cycles and its movements become more vigorous. This is an important milestone in fetal development as it indicates that brain and nervous system functions continue to mature.

The fetus now spends longer periods in sleep and wakefulness states. The mother may notice that the fetus is more active at certain times of the day, while it is calmer at other times. These cycles are part of the natural development of the fetus and can be affected by the mother's activities and routines.

The fetal kicks and movements become stronger and more noticeable during week 20. The mother can feel these kicks more clearly and also see them by observing her belly. It is important for the mother to note the movements and kicks of the fetus to ensure that the fetus is developing properly. If there are any changes in the movement pattern or if the mother feels worried, she should contact her doctor or midwife.

To support fetal sleep cycles and movements, the mother should continue to eat a nutritious diet and take her prenatal supplements. It is also important that the mother gets enough sleep and rest, as this can affect the well-being and development of the fetus.

Regular exercise is still important during week 20 of pregnancy, as long as it is safe and comfortable for the mother. Exercise can help maintain a healthy pregnancy and prepare the mother's body for childbirth.

Week 20 is an exciting time in pregnancy, when fetal sleep cycles and kicking become more noticeable. By eating a balanced diet, getting enough sleep and rest, and exercising regularly, the mother can help her baby develop and grow in the best possible way during this important time in life.

3.8. Week 21: Rapid growth of the brain

During week 21 of pregnancy, the fetal brain experiences a period of rapid growth and development. This is a critical time in fetal development because the brain coordinates all body functions and is responsible for cognition, behavior and personality.

The fetal brain develops continuously throughout pregnancy, but during week 21 there is a significant increase in the number of brain cells and their connections. These cells and connections will continue to develop and change after birth, but this rapid growth during pregnancy is critical to building the foundation for a healthy nervous system.

During this time, the fetus' sense of taste also begins to develop further, which means that it can taste what the mother eats through the amniotic fluid. This early exposure to different tastes can help shape the child's taste preferences later in life.

To support fetal brain development, it is important that the mother eats a nutritious diet, rich in omega-3 fatty acids, iron and folate. These nutrients play an important role in brain development and function. The mother should also continue to take her prenatal vitamins and avoid harmful substances, such as alcohol and tobacco, which can adversely affect the brain and nervous system of the fetus.

Getting enough sleep and managing stress in a healthy way is also important to support fetal brain development. The mother should strive to create a calm and relaxed environment and take time for relaxation and recovery.

Week 21 is a critical time for fetal brain development and growth. By eating a nutritious diet, avoiding harmful substances, sleeping and managing stress in a healthy way, the mother can help her child develop and grow in the best possible way during this important time in life.

3.9. Week 22: Hands and feet

During week 22 of pregnancy, the hands and feet of the fetus become more developed and detailed. At this point the fingers and toes have formed, and now the nails are starting to grow. The fetus also develops greater control over its movements, which means it can grasp, touch and explore its surroundings in the womb.

In addition, the fetus's sweat glands have begun to develop, which is an important part of the body's temperature regulation system. Sweating helps the body cool down when it is hot and is an important mechanism for maintaining a stable body temperature.

As the mother continues to feel the fetal movements and kicks more clearly during this time, she may also notice that the fetus becomes more active when she moves or changes position. This is normal and part of the natural development of the fetus.

To support the development of the fetus's hands and feet, it is important that the mother eats a nutritious diet, rich in vitamins and minerals that are necessary for the growth and development of the fetus. The mother should also continue to take her prenatal vitamins and avoid harmful substances, such as alcohol and tobacco, which can adversely affect fetal development.

Regular exercise is still important during week 22 of pregnancy, as long as it is safe and comfortable for the mother. Exercise helps maintain a healthy pregnancy and prepares the mother's body for childbirth.

Week 22 is an important time in fetal development, when hands and feet become more detailed and functional. By eating a balanced diet, taking care of her health and avoiding harmful substances, the mother can help her child develop and grow in the best possible way during this critical time in life.

3.10. Week 23: Breathing and fingerprints

During week 23 of pregnancy, the fetus begins to practice breathing movements and develops unique fingerprints. These milestones are important for the fetus's life outside the womb and help prepare it for the challenges that await after birth.

The fetus has now developed lungs that are mature enough to practice breathing movements, although they are not yet fully functional. By moving the chest and diaphragm, the fetus exercises the muscles needed to breathe after birth. These breathing movements also help strengthen the lungs and prepare them to function effectively after birth.

The fingerprints on the baby's fingertips also begin to form during week 23. These unique patterns are an important part of the baby's identity and are created by small ridges and pits in the skin. Fingerprints are unique to each individual and will remain unchanged throughout life.

To support fetal breathing movements and fingerprint development, it is important that the mother eats a nutritious diet and continues to take her prenatal vitamins. A balanced diet rich in vitamins, minerals and protein is necessary for fetal growth and development.

Regular exercise and good sleep are also important to support fetal development at week 23. The mother should aim to stay active, as long as it is safe and comfortable, and get enough rest to help the body recover and prepare for childbirth.

Week 23 is an exciting time in the development of the fetus, when it begins to practice breathing and develops its unique fingerprints. By eating a nutritious diet, exercising regularly and getting enough sleep, the mother can help her baby develop and grow in the best possible way during this important phase of life.

3.11. Week 24: Hearing and vision

During week 24 of pregnancy, the fetus's hearing and vision continue to develop, making it more receptive to sound and light. These advances are important for the fetus's ability to perceive and interact with its environment both in the womb and after birth.

The fetus's ear canals have opened up and it has begun to perceive sounds both from inside the mother's body and from the outside world. It can hear the mother's heartbeat, voice and digestion as well as sounds from the environment. Studies have shown that the fetus can respond to music, voices and other sound stimuli during this time, and certain sounds can even calm or stimulate the fetus.

Vision also develops during week 24, and the fetus's eyes are now sensitive to light. Although still limited in how much it can see, the fetus can perceive light and dark through the uterine wall. This early vision development helps prepare the fetus to be able to see and react to its surroundings after birth.

In order to support the hearing and vision development of the fetus, it is important that the mother eats a nutritious diet, rich in vitamins and minerals that are necessary for the growth and development of the fetus. The mother should also continue to take her prenatal vitamins and avoid harmful substances, such as alcohol and tobacco, which can adversely affect fetal development.

The mother can also start engaging her baby by talking, singing or playing music to it. These early interactions help build an emotional bond between mother and baby and can also have a calming effect on the fetus.

Week 24 is an important time in the development of the fetus, when its hearing and vision continue to develop and improve. By eating a nutritious diet, taking care of her health and engaging with her baby, the mother can help her baby develop and grow in the best possible way during this critical time in life.

3.12. Week 25: Obesity and blood vessels

During week 25 of pregnancy, the fetus develops an increased amount of body fat and its blood vessels become more complex. These changes are important to support the fetus's growing body and prepare it for life outside the womb.

The body fat that the fetus accumulates during this time acts as an energy reserve and helps to regulate body temperature. The fat also helps protect and support the internal organs and play a role in hormone production. A healthy amount of body fat is necessary for fetal survival and development.

The fetal vascular system continues to grow and become more complex, which is necessary to supply the rapidly growing body with oxygen and nutrients. The heart now pumps more blood through these vessels, providing the energy and nutrients needed to continue growing and developing.

To support the development of body fat and blood vessels in the fetus, it is important that the mother eats a nutritious diet, rich in healthy fats, proteins, vitamins and minerals. The mother should also continue to take her prenatal vitamins and avoid harmful substances, such as alcohol and tobacco, which can adversely affect fetal development.

Regular exercise is also important to maintain a healthy pregnancy and prepare the mother's body for childbirth. Exercise helps strengthen muscles, improve blood circulation and reduce the risk of complications during pregnancy and childbirth.

Week 25 is an important time in fetal development, when body fat and blood vessels continue to grow and develop. By eating a balanced diet, exercising regularly and avoiding harmful substances, the mother can help her child develop and grow in the best possible way during this critical time in life.

3.13. Week 26: Development of the immune system

During week 26 of pregnancy, the fetus's immune system begins to develop and become more active. This important development helps the fetus protect itself against infections and diseases both before and after birth.

The fetal immune system receives support and protection from the mother's immune system through the placenta. Antibodies developed by the mother are transferred to the fetus, giving it some protection against infections and diseases. This protection is called passive immunity and is essential for the survival of the fetus in the first months after birth.

During week 26, the fetus's own production of antibodies begins to increase, giving it a more active role in fighting infections and diseases. This active immunity continues to develop throughout pregnancy and becomes stronger after birth through breastfeeding, as the mother continues to transfer antibodies to her child.

To support the development of the fetus's immune system, it is important that the mother eats a nutritious diet, rich in vitamins and minerals that are necessary for the growth and development of the fetus. It is also important that the mother continues to take her prenatal vitamins and avoids exposure to infections or diseases that could harm the fetus.

Keeping up to date on recommended vaccines during pregnancy can also help protect both mother and fetus from potentially harmful diseases. Discussing any vaccinations and their safety with your doctor or midwife is important to ensure a healthy pregnancy and a safe start for the baby.

Week 26 is a critical time in the development of the fetus, when its immune system begins to develop and becomes more active. By eating a nutritious diet, taking care of her health and following vaccination recommendations, the mother can help her baby develop and grow in the best possible way during this important phase of life.

Third trimester: Weeks 27-40

During the third trimester, which extends from week 27 to 40, the pregnancy enters its final and crucial phase. The fetus continues to grow and mature in preparation for life outside the womb, and the mother prepares for childbirth. During this period, the fetus's organs continue to develop, and important physiological processes, such as the maturation of the brain and the ability of the lungs to breathe, reach important milestones.

The fetal brain and central nervous system develop rapidly during the third trimester, with increased complexity and the formation of new nerve cells and synapses. Myelination, a process in which nerve cells receive a protective insulation of fat and protein, takes place and helps speed up signal transmission between nerve cells. The mother's nutritional intake and lifestyle play an important role in the brain and nervous system development of the fetus, and it is important that she eats a nutritious diet and avoids exposure to harmful substances, such as alcohol and tobacco.

The fetus' lungs continue to develop and prepare to breathe after birth. The tiny air sacs in the lungs, called alveoli, begin to produce surfactant, a substance that helps prevent the lungs from collapsing when the baby takes its first breath. The fetus also begins to practice breathing by making rhythmic movements with the chest and diaphragm.

During the third trimester, the fetus also develops more regular sleep-wake cycles and gains more adipose tissue that helps it regulate body temperature after birth. In addition, the skeleton of the fetus continues to harden, and it gains more muscle mass and strength, which helps it move more vigorously and react to stimuli from the outside world.

Both the fetus' vision and hearing develop and improve during the third trimester. The fetus can now see light and shadows through the mother's abdomen, and it can hear and react to sounds from both the mother's body and the environment.

At the end of the third trimester, as the fetus nears full term, both the fetus and the mother prepare for delivery. The fetus usually begins to turn head down in preparation for birth, and the mother may experience cramping and other signs that the body is preparing for labor.

Throughout the third trimester, it is important for the mother to continue to eat a nutritious diet, take care of her health, and stay up to date on doctor appointments and recommended tests. This helps both mother and fetus to ensure a successful pregnancy and a healthy start in life.

Some of the most important aspects of the third trimester include fetal positioning, birth preparation, and parenting education. The mother may begin to feel the fetus move more forcefully and kick harder, which can be both exciting and uncomfortable. It is important to be aware of fetal movement patterns and to report any changes or decreases in movement to the health care provider, as this may be a sign that the fetus needs extra monitoring.

Birth preparation includes learning about the different stages of labor, pain relief, breathing techniques and when to go to the hospital or birthing clinic. It can be helpful to attend parenting classes or talk to friends and family who have been through childbirth to get a sense of what to expect.

Parenting education is another important part of the third trimester, as parents prepare to care for the newborn baby. Reading books, watching videos, and attending workshops on topics such as breastfeeding, infant care, sleep training, and home safety can be helpful.

It is also important to plan for parental leave and to prepare the home for the newborn baby by purchasing the necessary clothes, bedding, diapers and other equipment. Preparing mentally for the challenges and joys of parenthood is also an important part of the third trimester.

In summary, the third trimester is a time of rapid growth and development for the fetus as well as changes and preparations for the mother for childbirth. By taking care of their health, eating a nutritious diet, participating in parenting education and childbirth preparation, and maintaining open communication with the care provider, the mother and fetus can ensure a successful pregnancy and a healthy start in life.

4.1. Week 27: Balance and sleep

During week 27, fetal development continues, with a focus on balance and sleep. The fetus now begins to recognize certain positions and movements in the womb, which helps it develop a sense of balance and orientation. This is important so that the fetus can adapt to different body positions and movements as it grows and develops.

As the fetus's brain continues to mature, it begins to experience more regular sleep-wake cycles. It spends approximately 14-18 hours a day sleeping, which is crucial for its continued growth and development. During sleep, the fetus's brain and body get a chance to recover, and important processes such as cell growth and memory consolidation take place.

For the mother, the fetus's increased balance and sleeping habits mean that she may notice that the fetus's movements become more predictable and rhythmic. It is important for the mother to be aware of these movements and to report any changes or decreases in movements to her healthcare provider, as this may be a sign that the fetus needs extra monitoring.

To support the development of balance and sleep in the fetus, it is important that the mother continues to eat a nutritious diet and that she takes care of her own health and well-being. Avoiding stress and creating a calm and relaxed environment can also help promote healthy development for both mother and fetus.

The mother should also prepare for the fact that the movements of the fetus will become more powerful and clear during the third trimester. It's a good idea to talk to your healthcare provider about how to best manage and prepare for these changes, as well as discuss any questions or concerns that may arise during this time.

4.2. Week 28: Sight and breathing

During week 28, the fetus' vision continues to develop and improve. The retinas in the eyes become more sensitive to light and the fetus can begin to distinguish between light and dark. Although still limited in how much it can see, vision develops rapidly and helps the fetus prepare to see the world outside the womb.

At this time, the fetus also begins to practice breathing. The lungs are not fully developed yet, but the fetus can inhale and exhale small amounts of amniotic fluid, which helps strengthen the breathing muscles and prepare the lungs to function after birth. This breathing training is essential for the transition of the fetus from the womb to breathing air on its own after birth.

For the mother, this period in the development of the fetus means that she can feel the movements of the fetus more clearly and also notice some of its breathing exercises. It is important to pay attention to fetal movement patterns and to report any changes or decreases in movement to your health care provider.

To support the development of vision and breathing in the fetus, it is important that the mother continues to eat a nutritious diet and that she takes care of her own health and well-being. Avoiding stress and creating a calm and relaxed environment can also help promote healthy development for both mother and fetus.

During this time, it is also important for the mother to prepare for childbirth by attending parenting courses, reading about the childbirth process and discussing her expectations and wishes with her caregiver. Preparing mentally and physically for childbirth can make the transition to parenthood more positive and less stressful.

4.3. Week 29: Brain growth and skin protection

During week 29, the fetus's brain continues to grow and develop rapidly. Nerve cells and synapses are formed and strengthened, enabling the transfer of information between different parts of the brain and between the brain and the body. This rapid brain growth is crucial for the cognitive, motor and sensory development of the fetus both before and after birth.

At the same time, the skin of the fetus develops further to protect it from the surrounding environment. At this point, a waxy, cheese-like substance called vernix caseosa begins to form on the fetus's skin. Vernix acts as a barrier that protects the skin against irritation and infection and helps regulate body temperature. In addition, vernix acts as a natural lubricant that facilitates childbirth by making the body of the fetus more slippery as it passes through the birth canal.

For the mother, this phase in the development of the fetus means that she can feel the movements of the fetus even more clearly and also notice that the fetus reacts more to external stimuli, such as sound and touch. It is important to pay attention to fetal movement patterns and to report any changes or decreases in movement to your health care provider.

To support fetal brain growth and skin development, it is important that the mother continues to eat a nutritious diet, rich in omega-3 fatty acids and other essential nutrients. It is also important that the mother takes care of her own health and well-being by avoiding stress, getting enough sleep and creating a calm and relaxed environment for both herself and the fetus.

During this time, it is also important for the mother to continue preparing for childbirth and parenthood by attending parenting classes, reading about the birth process, and discussing her expectations and wishes with her caregiver. Preparing mentally and physically for childbirth can make the transition to parenthood more positive and less stressful.

4.4. Week 30: The skeletal system and fetal weight gain

During week 30, the fetal skeletal system continues to strengthen and prepares for life outside the womb. Cartilage turns into bone, and the bones become harder and stronger. This is an important process to ensure that the fetus will be able to support its own body weight and perform movements after birth.

During this period, the weight of the fetus also increases rapidly. Fat accumulates around the body to insulate and protect vital organs, helping to regulate body temperature and acting as an energy reserve after birth. This weight gain is critical to the health and well-being of the fetus and helps ensure a smooth transition to life outside the womb.

For the mother, the skeletal and weight development of the fetus means that she can feel an increased weight and load on her body. It is important that she listens to her body and adjusts her activity level and sleep as needed. She should also continue to eat a nutritious diet to support fetal growth and development.

Carrying a growing baby can also lead to back pain and other discomfort for the mother. It is important that she discuss these concerns with her healthcare provider and explore strategies to manage the pain, such as participating in pregnancy yoga, using a support belt, or getting massages.

To prepare for childbirth and parenthood, the mother should continue to attend parenting classes, read about the birth process, and discuss her expectations and wishes with her health care provider. Preparing mentally and physically for childbirth can make the transition to parenthood more positive and less stressful.

4.5. Week 31: Lung development and fetal sleep

During week 31, the fetus' lungs continue to develop and prepare to breathe air after birth. The fetus's lungs are now better equipped to produce surfactant, a substance that helps prevent the lungs from collapsing as they expand and contract during breathing. This development is crucial to ensure that the fetus will be able to breathe independently after birth.

At the same time, the fetus begins to establish more regular sleep patterns and experiences periods of activity and rest. It is common for the mother to feel these movements and rest as part of the fetus's daily routine. It is important to pay attention to fetal movement patterns and to report any changes or decreases in movement to your health care provider.

To support fetal lung development and sleep, it is important that the mother continues to eat a nutritious diet and take care of her own health and well-being. Avoiding stress and creating a calm and relaxed environment can also help promote healthy development for both mother and fetus.

During this time, it is also important for the mother to continue preparing for childbirth and parenthood by attending parenting classes, reading about the birth process, and discussing her expectations and wishes with her caregiver. Preparing mentally and physically for childbirth can make the transition to parenthood more positive and less stressful.

4.6. Week 32: Visual acuity and movement coordination

During week 32, the fetus' visual acuity and the ability to focus on objects improve. Although the fetus' vision is limited inside the womb, it can now perceive light and dark and react to changes in light intensity. These early visual experiences are important for the future visual development of the fetus and help it prepare to perceive the outside world after birth.

The fetus's movement coordination also continues to develop during this period. The fetus can now move its limbs more smoothly and in a coordinated manner, making it possible to perform more complex movements, such as grasping, kicking and turning. These movements are important for the motor development of the fetus and help it to strengthen and train its muscles for life outside the womb.

For the mother, the development of the fetus' vision and movement means that she can feel more powerful kicks and movements, and she can even notice that the fetus reacts to external stimuli, such as light and sound. It is important to pay attention to fetal movement patterns and to report any changes or decreases in movement to your health care provider.

In order to support the development of the fetus' vision and movement, it is important that the mother continues to eat a nutritious diet and takes care of her own health and well-being. Avoiding stress and creating a calm and relaxed environment can also help promote healthy development for both mother and fetus.

During this time, it is also important for the mother to continue preparing for childbirth and parenthood by attending parenting classes, reading about the birth process, and discussing her expectations and wishes with her caregiver. Preparing mentally and physically for childbirth can make the transition to parenthood more positive and less stressful.

4.7. Week 33: Brain development and fetal position

During week 33, the fetal brain continues to develop rapidly, with increased brain activity and the formation of new nerve connections. These changes are essential to support the fetus's cognitive, motor and sensory development and prepare it to learn and interact with the outside world after birth.

At the same time, the fetus begins to prepare for birth by assuming a more optimal position in the uterus. Most fetuses are head down at this point, although some may still be in the breech position (where the bottom or feet are down). If the fetus is still in the breech position at this time, the provider may recommend certain exercises or techniques to encourage the fetus to turn into the correct position for delivery.

For the mother, it is important to continue eating a nutritious diet and to take care of her own health and well-being to support fetal brain development and preparation for birth. Avoiding stress and creating a calm and relaxed environment can also help promote healthy development for both mother and fetus.

During this time, it is also important for the mother to continue preparing for childbirth and parenthood by attending parenting classes, reading about the birth process, and discussing her expectations and wishes with her caregiver. Preparing mentally and physically for childbirth can make the transition to parenthood more positive and less stressful.

4.8. Week 34: Maturation of the immune system and preparation for breastfeeding

During week 34, the fetus's immune system continues to mature and prepares to fight infections and diseases after birth. The fetus receives antibodies from the mother through the placenta, which helps it build up its own immune system. This transfer of antibodies is particularly important to protect the newborn against infections during the first months of life.

For the mother, it is important to continue to eat a nutritious diet and take care of her own health and well-being to support the fetus's immune system. Keeping up to date on recommended vaccinations during pregnancy can also help protect both mother and fetus from infections and diseases.

During this period, mammary glands also begin to prepare for breastfeeding. The breasts may become larger and heavier, and it is possible that the mother may experience leakage of colostrum, the first milk produced after birth. Colostrum is very nutritious and contains important antibodies that help protect the newborn against infections.

To prepare for breastfeeding, the mother can read about breastfeeding techniques, attend breastfeeding classes, and talk to her health care provider or a breastfeeding expert about any questions or concerns. Feeling safe and prepared before breastfeeding can contribute to a positive breastfeeding experience for both mother and baby.

During this time, it is also important for the mother to continue preparing for childbirth and parenthood by attending parenting classes, reading about the birth process, and discussing her expectations and wishes with her caregiver. Preparing mentally and physically for childbirth can make the transition to parenthood more positive and less stressful.

4.9. Week 35: Weight gain and maturation of the lungs

During week 35, the fetus continues to gain weight and prepares for life outside the womb. Fat reserves are stored to help the fetus regulate its body temperature and provide energy after birth. These fat reserves also contribute to the increased weight of the fetus, which helps it develop muscle strength and motor skills.

The lungs also continue to mature during this period, and the fetus begins to produce surfactant – a substance that helps prevent the lungs from collapsing as they expand and contract during breathing. This maturation of the lungs is essential to ensure that the fetus will be able to breathe independently after birth.

For the mother, the fetus' weight gain and lung maturation mean that she can feel increased weight and pressure in the pelvic area, which can lead to increased fatigue and discomfort. It is important that the mother continues to rest and take care of her own health and well-being during this period.

To support fetal weight gain and lung maturation, it is important that the mother continues to eat a nutritious diet and gets enough rest. Avoiding stress and creating a calm and relaxed environment can also help promote healthy development for both mother and fetus.

During this time, it is also important for the mother to continue preparing for childbirth and parenthood by attending parenting classes, reading about the birth process, and discussing her expectations and wishes with her caregiver. Preparing mentally and physically for childbirth can make the transition to parenthood more positive and less stressful.

4.10. Week 36: Full term and preparations for childbirth

When week 36 begins, the fetus is considered full-term, meaning it is developed enough to survive outside the womb with minimal medical assistance. Although the fetus still continues to grow and develop during the remaining weeks of pregnancy, its organs and systems are now mature enough for life outside the womb.

During this period, the fetus continues to increase in weight and size, which means that there may be less room for movement inside the uterus. The mother may notice that fetal movements feel more limited and less vigorous than before, but it is important to continue to monitor fetal movements and report any changes to the health care provider.

To prepare for the birth, the mother and her partner or support person should begin to discuss and plan for the birth. This can mean creating a birth plan, packing a bag for the hospital stay, and preparing the home for the baby's arrival. By being well prepared, the mother and her partner can feel more secure and less stressed as labor approaches.

It is important that the mother continues to look after her own health and well-being during this period, by eating a nutritious diet, getting enough rest and avoiding stress. Creating a calm and relaxed environment can also help promote healthy development for both mother and fetus.

During this time, it is also important for the mother to continue preparing for childbirth and parenthood by attending parenting classes, reading about the birth process, and discussing her expectations and wishes with her caregiver. Preparing mentally and physically for childbirth can make the transition to parenthood more positive and less stressful.

4.11. Week 37: Baby's position and preparation for birth

When week 37 begins, the baby begins to position itself for the birth. Most babies turn head down in the womb, which is called head presentation. This is the most common and safest position for birth, but it is important to note that some babies may be in the breech position (butt or feet down) or in another position. If the baby is in the breech position, the provider may attempt to turn the baby manually through a technique called external cephalic version (ECV), or discuss alternative delivery methods, such as cesarean section, with the mother.

To facilitate the baby's movement and positioning before delivery, the mother can continue to be physically active, by going for walks, doing pregnancy-adapted exercise or practicing prenatal yoga. It is also important that the mother follow the health care provider's advice regarding safe and effective methods of encouraging the baby's positioning.

During this period, the mother's body also begins to prepare for childbirth. This can mean that the cervix begins to soften, thin and dilate, allowing the baby to pass through the birth canal. Some women may also experience contractions, which are irregular contractions that help prepare the uterus for labor.

To prepare for the birth, it is important that the mother and her partner or support person continue to attend parenting courses, read about the birth process and discuss their expectations and wishes with their healthcare provider. Being well prepared can contribute to a more positive and less stressful birth experience.

It is also important that the mother continues to look after her own health and well-being during this period, by eating a nutritious diet, getting enough rest and avoiding stress. Creating a calm and relaxed environment can also help promote healthy development for both mother and baby.

4.12. Week 38: Birth weight and feelings before childbirth

As week 38 approaches, the baby continues to put on weight for delivery. Fat reserves are built up to help the baby regulate its body temperature and provide energy after birth. Average birth weight for a full-term child varies, but is usually between 2.5 and 4.5 kg. However, it is important to remember that the baby's weight at birth can vary depending on many factors, such as the mother's health, genetics and length of pregnancy.

During this period, the mother may experience a range of emotions before the upcoming birth. It is normal to feel excitement, nervousness, worry and anticipation. In order to manage these feelings, it is important that the mother and her partner or support person communicate openly and honestly about their feelings and expectations before the birth.

To prepare for the birth, the mother and her partner or support person can continue to attend parenting classes, read about the birth process, and discuss their expectations and wishes with their caregiver. Being well prepared can contribute to a more positive and less stressful birth experience.

It is also important that the mother continues to look after her own health and well-being during this period, by eating a nutritious diet, getting enough rest and avoiding stress. Creating a calm and relaxed environment can also help promote healthy development for both mother and baby.

At this stage, it is also important that the mother and her partner or support person are ready to go to the labor ward when the time comes. Make sure the bag for the hospital stay is packed, and that you have a plan for transport to the hospital.

4.13. Week 39: Checkups and signs of labor

As week 39 begins, it is very close to delivery, and the mother is likely to visit her health care provider more often to monitor both her own and the baby's health. The caregiver can check the maturity and position of the cervix, as well as the baby's position and heart sounds. These checks help assess whether labor is close and whether there are any potential complications to be aware of.

During this period, it is important to pay attention to signs of labor, such as:

1. Contractions: Regular and increasing contractions that are getting stronger and closer together are a sign that labor may have started.

2. Water loss: If the amniotic fluid leaks or runs, it may be a sign that labor is near.

3. Bloody discharge: A bloody mucus plug can dislodge from the cervix and be a sign that labor is about to begin.

4. Decrease in the baby's movements: If the baby's movements decrease drastically or stop completely, contact the caregiver immediately.

If any of these signs appear, the mother and her partner or support person should contact the health care provider or go to the labor ward to assess the situation and get the right care.

To prepare for the birth, it is important that the mother and her partner or support person continue to attend parenting courses, read about the birth process and discuss their expectations and wishes with their healthcare provider. Being well prepared can contribute to a more positive and less stressful birth experience.

It is also important that the mother continues to look after her own health and well-being during this period, by eating a nutritious diet, getting enough rest and avoiding stress. Creating a calm and relaxed environment can also help promote healthy development for both mother and baby.

4.14. Week 40: Estimated due date and gestational age

When week 40 arrives, it's time for the estimated due date. It is important to remember that this date is only an estimate and that only about 5% of all babies are born on the exact estimated due date. Many babies are born a few days before or after this date, and this is completely normal.

If week 40 passes without any signs of labor, the mother will be considered over-pregnant. It is not uncommon for a first pregnancy to go over time, and up to 10% of all pregnancies may be overterm. During this time, the health care provider will monitor the health of the mother and baby closely and may suggest methods to encourage labor to begin, such as acupuncture, acupressure or membrane sweep.

If labor has not started within a week or two of the estimated due date, the health care provider may discuss the possibility of inducing labor. Induction can be done for medical reasons, such as if the mother has high blood pressure, if the baby is not growing as expected, or if the amniotic fluid has decreased. Induction may also be considered if the mother is very uncomfortable or worried about being overburdened.

During this period, it is important that the mother continues to take care of her own health and well-being, by eating a nutritious diet, getting enough rest and avoiding stress. Creating a calm and relaxed environment can also help promote healthy development for both mother and baby. Preparations for the birth and the first few days with the newborn, such as having a plan for transport to the hospital and a packed bag for the hospital stay, should be in place by now.

Preparations for childbirth and the first time at home

When the pregnancy is nearing its end and childbirth is at the door, it is important to prepare both practically and mentally for the big change that is to come. This period is filled with anticipation, but can also raise concerns and many questions. By preparing well for the birth and the first time at home with the newborn baby, you can create a secure foundation for your new life as a parent.

One of the most important aspects of preparing for childbirth is creating a birth plan. A birth plan is a way for the mother and her partner or support person to communicate their wishes and expectations before the birth to the care provider. This may include preferences regarding pain relief, who should be present during the birth, what position the mother wants to give birth in and any wishes regarding umbilical cord removal and skin-to-skin contact after birth. Drawing up a birth plan together with your partner or support person can be a good way to discuss expectations, fears and wishes before the birth. Remember that a birth plan is a tool for communication and that it is important to be open to change, as births do not always follow the plan.

It is also important to participate in parenting courses to gain knowledge about childbirth, the baby's first period, breastfeeding and parenting. Parenting courses can help parents-to-be feel more prepared and confident before childbirth and life with the newborn baby. The courses often offer both theoretical and practical knowledge on topics such as childbirth techniques, the child's needs, sleep, breastfeeding and the role of parents. Participating in parenting courses together with your partner or support person can strengthen the bond between you and provide a common basis for future parenthood.

Preparing the home for the arrival of the newborn baby is also an important part of the preparations. This means ensuring that there is a safe and welcoming environment for the child to come home to. This may mean purchasing necessary supplies, such as clothes, diapers, a bed for the baby and other important things. It is also good to think about creating a calm and relaxed atmosphere in the home, by preparing a place for breastfeeding or bottle feeding and a place where you can change diapers and take care of the child's hygiene.

The first time at home with the newborn baby can be both wonderful and challenging. It is a period of adjustment for the whole family and a time when the parents get to know their child and its needs. Being prepared that the child's sleeping and eating habits may vary and that it may take time before routines are established can help parents manage expectations during this period.

To facilitate this adjustment period, it is important to ask for help and support from family, friends and caregivers. New parents need time to rest, recover and bond with their baby. Asking for help with practical things, such as cooking, washing and cleaning, can give parents more time and energy to focus on their child and their own needs.

It is also important to take care of your own health and well-being during this time. Eating a nutritious diet, drinking enough water and trying to get as much sleep as possible are important factors for parents to be at their best for their child. Taking care of your own mental health is also important, and talking to someone about feelings and experiences can help process and manage the changes that parenthood brings.

It is also a good idea to create a list of important phone numbers and contacts to keep close at hand in case of questions or emergencies. This list may include telephone numbers for midwives, BVC, children's emergency room, insurance fund and other relevant information.

Finally, remember that every parent and child is unique and there is no perfect parenting manual. It is normal to feel insecure and to make mistakes. The most important thing is to be open to learning, to adapt to the child's needs and to seek support and advice from others when needed. In this way, you and your child will grow and develop together and create a strong and loving relationship.

5.1. Birth planning

Birth planning is an important part of the preparations for the baby's arrival. A birth plan is a document in which the mother-to-be and her partner or support person write down their wishes and expectations before the birth. The purpose of the plan is to facilitate communication between the woman giving birth, her partner and the healthcare staff during childbirth.

The following aspects can be considered when preparing a birth plan:

1. Pain relief: What types of pain relief does the laboring woman desire? There are many different options, such as epidural anesthesia, nitrous oxide, sterile water injections and acupuncture. It is important to understand the risks and benefits of each method and to be open to changing the plan if the situation calls for it.

2. Birth positions: What positions does the birthing woman feel comfortable in? It can be lying down, sitting, standing or on all fours. Discuss different positions and their advantages and disadvantages with the nursing staff.

3. Birth partner: Who should be present during the birth? It could be a partner, a friend, a family member or a doula. Think about how these people can provide support and help during the birth.

4. Umbilical cord cutting: When should the umbilical cord be cut? Some families prefer to wait until the umbilical cord has stopped pulsating, while others desire an immediate de-navel. Discuss options with healthcare professionals and make a decision based on scientific advice and personal preference.

5. Skin-to-skin contact: Skin-to-skin contact between the newborn and the mother or partner is important to promote attachment and regulate the baby's body temperature and heart rate. Enter in the birth plan when and for how long skin-to-skin contact is desired after the birth.

6. Breastfeeding: If the mother plans to breastfeed, write in the plan that she wants to start breastfeeding as soon as possible after the birth and that she wants support from the nursing staff if needed.

It is important to remind yourself that a birth plan is a tool for communication and that it is important to be flexible. Births are unpredictable, and the plan may need to be adjusted during the process. Being open to changes and having an open dialogue with the healthcare staff can contribute to a positive birth experience.

5.2. Preparations for childbirth

Preparation for childbirth involves gathering information, planning and preparing both mentally and physically for the upcoming event. Here are some things to keep in mind as you prepare for childbirth:

1. Antenatal class: Attend an antenatal class, either online or on-site, to learn about pregnancy, childbirth and parenting. The course can help you build confidence and learn techniques to manage pain and stress during labour.

2. Breathing Techniques: Learn different breathing techniques that can help you relax and focus during labor. Deep breathing, slow breathing and modified breathing are some examples of techniques that can be used.

3. Physical activity: Continue to be physically active during pregnancy, if possible. It can help improve your endurance, strength and flexibility, which can be beneficial during labor. Consult your doctor before starting any new exercise routine.

4. Relaxation techniques: Learn relaxation techniques, such as meditation, mindfulness, or progressive muscle relaxation, to help you manage stress and anxiety before labor.

5. Pack a baby bag: Prepare a bag with essential items for the birth and time in the hospital. Include clothes for you and your newborn, toiletries, nursing pillow, snacks, camera and charger, as well as important documents and phone numbers.

6. Create a supportive environment: Plan for a calm and relaxing environment during labor. You can consider bringing objects that give you security and relaxation, such as music, scented candles, pillows or blankets.

7. Get support from a doula: A doula is a professional birth attendant who offers emotional, physical, and informational support during pregnancy, labor, and postpartum. If you are interested in hiring a doula, start looking early to find one that fits you and your needs.

By preparing for childbirth, you can feel more confident and ready to face the challenges and joys that lie ahead. Remember that every birth is unique and that it is important to be flexible and open to changes during the process.

5.3. Things to think about after giving birth

After childbirth, it is important to focus on recovery, both physical and emotional, as well as taking care of the newborn baby. Here are some things to keep in mind after giving birth:

1. Skin-to-skin contact: Continue skin-to-skin contact between the newborn and the parents to promote attachment, regulate the baby's body temperature and heart rate, and facilitate breastfeeding.

2. Breastfeeding: If you plan to breastfeed, start as soon as possible after delivery. Ask for help and support from healthcare professionals if you need it, and don't hesitate to seek professional help from a breastfeeding expert if you have problems or questions.

3. Sleep Cycles: Be prepared for the newborn baby to have irregular sleep cycles in the first few weeks. Try to sleep when the baby sleeps and ask for help from your partner, family or friends to share the responsibility and get rest.

4. Recovery for the mother: Take care of yourself and your body after childbirth. It can take time to recover physically and emotionally, so give yourself time and space to rest and recover. If you experience pain, bleeding or other symptoms that worry you, contact your doctor or midwife for advice and help.

5. Routines and habits: Try to create routines and habits that will help you deal with the new challenges of parenthood. This can mean planning for meals, cleaning and taking care of household chores, as well as finding time to relax and enjoy moments together with your partner and your child.

6. Emotional support: Parenting can be both rewarding and challenging, and it's important to have emotional support from your partner, family and friends. If you're feeling overwhelmed, stressed, or experiencing signs of postpartum depression, don't hesitate to seek professional help.

7. Parenting groups and networks: Join parenting groups and networks to meet other parents, share experiences and get support and advice. Being part of a parenting group can help reduce feelings of isolation and stress that can occur in the first few months of parenthood.

Being prepared for the changes and challenges after giving birth can help you feel more confident and ready to take care of your newborn and yourself. Remember that it's normal to feel overwhelmed and unsure at times, and that it's important to ask for help and support when needed.

5.4. Newborn examinations and vaccinations

It is important to follow up with regular examinations and vaccinations to ensure that your child is growing and developing properly. Here are some key points to consider:

1. First examination: The first examination of your newborn child, also called the newborn examination, is usually

carried out within 24 hours after delivery. This examination includes a careful assessment of the child's heart, lungs, skin, reflexes, hearing, vision, and more.

2. Follow-up visits: Regular follow-up visits to the midwife or pediatrician are important to monitor your child's growth and development. During these visits, the caregiver will measure your child's height, weight, and head circumference, as well as evaluate developmental milestones.

3. Hearing screening: A hearing screening is recommended for all newborn babies, usually before they leave the hospital. If your baby doesn't get a hearing screening at the hospital, make sure to schedule one within the first few weeks after the birth.

4. PKU test: A PKU test (phenylketonuria test) is usually performed on all newborn babies within the first few days after birth. This blood test tests for several inherited diseases, including phenylketonuria, which can cause serious health problems if not detected and treated early.

5. Vaccinations: Follow the recommended vaccination program to protect your child against serious diseases. The first vaccinations are usually given at 2 months of age, but some vaccinations may be given earlier depending on your child's health and risk factors.

6. Vitamin K: A Vitamin K supplement is recommended for all newborn babies, as it helps prevent a rare but serious bleeding disorder called vitamin K deficiency bleeding.

By following up with regular examinations and vaccinations, you can ensure that your child gets the best possible start in life and that any health problems are detected and treated early. It is important to communicate with your healthcare provider and ask questions if you have any concerns or need additional information about your child's health and development.

5.5. Take care of yourself as a parent

Becoming a parent often means focusing on your child's needs and well-being, but it's also important to take care of yourself to be a good parent. Here are some tips to take care of yourself during this new phase of your life:

1. Create a balance between work and leisure: It is important to find a balance between work, parenting and personal time. Creating a routine and planning to share parenting responsibilities with your partner or other family members can help you find that balance.

2. Eat healthy: Be sure to eat a nutritious diet that will give you energy and support your postpartum recovery. This is especially important if you are breastfeeding, as your body needs extra nutrients to produce milk.

3. Exercise regularly: Regular exercise can help relieve stress, increase energy levels and support your physical and mental health. Consult your doctor before starting any postpartum exercise routine and start slowly.

4. Sleep: Sleep is an important part of your health and recovery, but getting enough sleep with a newborn can be difficult. Try to sleep when the baby sleeps and ask for help from your partner, family or friends to share the night wakings.

5. Emotional support: If you're feeling overwhelmed or experiencing signs of postpartum depression, seek professional help and talk to your partner, family and friends about your feelings. It is important to have emotional support during this transition period.

6. Time for yourself: Make time for yourself and your interests to recharge your batteries and promote your mental health. It can be something as simple as reading a book, going for a walk or seeing friends.

7. Communicate with your partner: Keep open communication with your partner about your feelings, needs and expectations about parenting. It is important to support and help each other during this transition period.

By taking care of yourself and prioritizing your own health and well-being, you can become a more present, loving and effective parent to your child. Remember that it's okay to ask for help and support when needed, and that it's normal to feel overwhelmed and unsure at times.

5.6. Create a safe and supportive environment for your child

Creating a safe and supportive environment for your child is an important part of parenting. Here are some tips for creating such an environment:

1. Child safety in the home: Make sure your home is child-proof by installing safety gates at stairs, using corner protectors on furniture, securing large furniture to the wall and locking cupboards containing hazardous substances. Make sure all small objects and choking hazards are out of your child's reach.

2. Safe sleep: Follow safe sleep recommendations, including placing your baby on their back to sleep, using a firm mattress without pillows or loose blankets, and not sharing a bed with your baby. Also make sure the bedroom is cool and well ventilated.

3. Child-safe car: Make sure your child is always safe in the car by using an age- and size-appropriate car seat and following the manufacturer's installation instructions. Always lock the car when not in use and keep car keys out of your child's reach.

4. Supportive and loving interaction: Create an environment where your child feels loved and supported by showing love and closeness, encouraging and praising your child, and engaging in positive communication. This includes talking, singing, reading and playing together.

5. Routines and structure: Create a daily routine for your child with regular meals, sleep and activities. This helps your child to feel safe and to develop good habits.

6. Social and emotional skills: Encourage your child to develop social and emotional skills by interacting with other children and adults, talking about feelings and behaviors, and teaching your child to express themselves in healthy ways.

7. Learning and development: Create opportunities for your child to explore, learn and develop by offering a range of stimulating activities and toys that suit your child's age and interests. This includes activities such as drawing, building, singing, dancing and playing outside.

By creating a safe and supportive environment for your child, you can help them develop and flourish physically, emotionally and cognitively. Remember that parenting is an ongoing process and that it is important to adapt to your child's growing needs.

5.7. After birth: Caring for your newborn baby

Caring for your newborn can be an overwhelming experience, but there are some basic things you can do to help your baby adjust to life outside the womb:

1. Follow the recommendations for safe sleep: Make sure your child sleeps on their back in a safe sleeping environment without loose blankets, pillows or soft toys. Also, do not place your child in the same bed as you.

2. Feed your baby regularly: Newborns need to be fed often, usually every 2-3 hours. Breastfeeding or bottle feeding are good options to give your baby the nutrition it needs.

3. Keep your baby clean: Wash your baby's body regularly and change diapers often to keep your baby clean and comfortable.

4. Avoid overstimulating your baby: Newborns are sensitive to too much stimulation, so avoid too much noise, light and movement around your baby.

5. Be patient: It takes time to adjust to life with a newborn and it's normal to feel unsure or overwhelmed. Be patient with yourself and seek support from your partner, friends and family.

6. Keep in regular contact with your doctor: Your doctor can help monitor your baby's health and development, and give you advice on how to best care for your baby.

Caring for a newborn can be challenging, but it is also one of the most rewarding experiences in life. By providing your child with a safe and loving environment, you can help support their development and health.

5.8. Aftercare for the mother after childbirth

Aftercare for the mother after childbirth is as important as caring for the newborn baby. Here are some important things to keep in mind:

1. Physical recovery: After giving birth, the body may take time to recover. Make sure you give your body enough rest, eat healthy and avoid heavy lifting and strenuous activities.

2. Mental health: After giving birth, it can be common to feel overwhelmed, anxious or depressed. Be open with your partner, family and healthcare professionals about how you are feeling and seek help if you need it.

3. Breastfeeding: If you plan to breastfeed, make sure you get support and advice from healthcare professionals or a lactation consultant to get breastfeeding off to a good start.

4. Check your body: Make sure you follow up with your doctor and do the necessary tests to make sure your body is recovering properly after giving birth.

5. Support from partner and environment: After childbirth, it can be difficult to manage everything on your own. Seek

support from your partner, family and friends to help with daily work and give you opportunities for recovery and rest.

Aftercare is an important part of recovery after childbirth. By taking care of yourself, you can better take care of your child and give them the best possible start in life.

5.9. Returning to everyday life after childbirth

Returning to everyday life after childbirth can be a big challenge, both physically and emotionally. Here are some things to keep in mind to make the transition smoother:

1. Take it easy: Give yourself time to recover and return to everyday life at your own pace. It is important not to push yourself too much and to give yourself enough time to recover.

2. Seek support: Seek support from your partner, family and friends. It can be helpful to ask for help with household chores, cooking or child care to reduce stress.

3. Plan ahead: Plan ahead to ease the transition back into everyday life. Consider things like breastfeeding needs, childcare and creating a routine that works for you and your family.

4. Focus on your health: Focus on taking care of yourself and your health by eating healthy foods, exercising regularly and getting enough sleep.

5. Be realistic: Be realistic with your expectations and goals. You may not be able to do everything you used to

do in the same way as before and that is completely
normal.

Returning to everyday life after giving birth can be a challenge,
but it is also an opportunity to get to know your newborn baby
and create a closer relationship with your partner. By taking it
easy and focusing on your health and well-being, you can give
yourself and your family the best possible start to this new phase
of life.

5.10. Returning to work after childbirth

Returning to work after giving birth can be a big challenge, both emotionally and practically. Here are some things to keep in mind to make the transition smoother:

1. Plan ahead: Plan ahead to ease the transition back to work. Think about things like childcare, breastfeeding needs and creating a routine that works for you and your family.

2. Be realistic: Be realistic about your expectations and goals when returning to work. You may not be able to do everything you used to do in the same way as before and that is completely normal.

3. Seek support: Seek support from your employer and colleagues to facilitate your return to work. Ask for flexible working hours or opportunities to work from home if needed.

4. Take care of yourself: Continue to take care of yourself by eating healthy foods, exercising regularly and getting enough sleep. This will help you manage the stress that may arise when you return to work.

5. Set boundaries: Set boundaries to maintain a balance between work and family life. Finding a balance can be difficult, but setting limits on work and leisure time can help reduce stress and give you more time to focus on your family.

Returning to work after childbirth can be a challenge, but it is also an opportunity to continue to develop your career and maintain a balance between work and family life. By planning ahead and seeking support, you can make the transition smoother and continue to take care of yourself and your family.

5.11. Dealing with the challenges of parenthood

Being a parent is one of the most challenging and rewarding tasks in life. Here are some of the most common challenges parents can face and how to deal with them:

1. Lack of sleep: Lack of sleep is a common challenge for new parents. To manage it, it can be helpful to take short naps during the day, enlist the help of a partner or another adult to care for the baby, or create a routine to facilitate sleep at night.

2. Breastfeeding: Breastfeeding can be a challenge for new mothers. It may be helpful to seek support from lactation consultants or other mothers, create a relaxing breastfeeding environment, or consider pumping as an alternative.

3. Lack of time: Finding time for yourself or for relationships can be difficult for new parents. To manage this, it can be helpful to create a routine that works for the whole family, ask for help from a partner or another adult, or plan a regular "data night" or time for self-care.

4. Finding a balance between work and family: Finding a balance between work and family can be a challenge for many parents. To manage this, it can be helpful to seek

support from employers or colleagues, set clear boundaries for working hours and leisure time, or consider flexible working hours or working from home if possible.

5. Emotional challenges: Emotional challenges, such as anxiety, stress and depression, are common for new parents. It is important to seek support from a partner, friends or professionals, and to take care of your own physical and emotional health.

Being a parent can be challenging, but it can also be one of the most fulfilling and rewarding tasks in life. By seeking support, creating a routine that works for the whole family, and taking care of their own health and well-being, parents can overcome the challenges that may arise and enjoy their new role as a parent.

5.12. Enjoying parenthood

Enjoying parenthood is about taking the time to appreciate the little moments and make memories that last a lifetime. Here are some things to keep in mind to help you enjoy parenthood:

1. Create memories: Create memories by taking photos, recording videos or writing diaries about your child's development and milestones.

2. Play and explore: Play and explore with your child by participating in activities that suit their age and interests. This can include reading books, painting, playing games, or going on outdoor adventures.

3. Create a routine: Create a routine that works for the whole family and allows time for both work and leisure. This can help you appreciate and enjoy the small moments in life.

4. Create a support group: Create a support group of other parents or family members who can provide support and share experiences with.

5. Take care of yourself: Take care of your own physical and emotional health by eating healthy foods, exercising regularly and getting enough sleep. This will help you enjoy parenthood more and cope with the challenges that may arise.

Enjoying parenthood is about making memories and appreciating the small moments in life. By creating a routine that works for the whole family, seeking support from other parents or family members, and taking care of their own health and well-being, parents can enjoy the unique and fulfilling experience of raising a child.

5.13. Dealing with changes in the relationship

Parenthood can affect the relationship between two people in many ways. It is important to manage these changes and find ways to continue building a strong and loving relationship. Here are some things to consider:

1. Communication: Communication is the key to a strong and healthy relationship. It is important to talk openly and honestly about one's feelings, needs and expectations.

2. Make time for each other: Make time for each other and find ways to do things together that you both enjoy. It can be as simple as having a "data night" once a week or going for a walk together.

3. Forgiveness: Parenting can be stressful and challenging, and it can lead to conflicts and misunderstandings. It is important to be able to forgive each other and work together to solve problems.

4. Support each other: Supporting each other and showing appreciation is important to building a strong relationship. Show your partner that you appreciate everything they do and be there for them when they need it.

5. Seek help if needed: If the relationship is in crisis or you need help coping with the changes that parenthood brings, don't hesitate to seek professional help.

Parenthood can be challenging for a relationship, but it can also be an opportunity to build a stronger and more loving relationship. By communicating openly and honestly, making time for each other, forgiving each other, supporting each other and seeking help if needed, parents can manage the changes that parenthood brings and continue to build a strong and healthy relationship.

After childbirth: Care of the newborn and breastfeeding

After the birth, it is important to give the newborn the right care and nutrition. Here are some things to keep in mind when it comes to caring for your newborn and breastfeeding:

1. Breast milk or formula: Breast milk is the best source of nutrition for the newborn. If you cannot or choose to breastfeed, you can use breast milk substitute.

2. Breastfeeding: Breastfeeding can be a challenge for some women and it is important to get support and advice from a lactation consultant or midwife. Breastfeeding is not only a source of nutrition for the newborn, it can also strengthen the bond between mother and baby and provide benefits for the mother such as a reduced risk of breast cancer.

3. Skin-to-skin contact: Skin-to-skin contact is important for creating a close relationship between parent and child and can also help the newborn regulate body temperature and breathing.

4. Sleep: The newborn sleeps a lot and needs regular sleep to grow and develop. It is important to try to get enough sleep yourself and to let the newborn sleep when they need it.

5. Attention to signs of illness: The newborn is more susceptible to illness and infection, so it is important to be alert to signs of illness and seek medical attention if necessary.

Caring for a newborn can be challenging, but there are many resources and supports to help. Giving the newborn the right care and nutrition is important for their growth and development, and getting support and advice from a lactation consultant or midwife can help with breastfeeding. Skin-to-skin contact is also an important part of creating a close relationship between parent and child.

6.1. Care of the umbilical cord

The umbilical cord is the one that connects the newborn to the placenta in the womb and transports nutrition and oxygen. After delivery, it is important to take care of the umbilical cord to avoid infections. Here are some things to keep in mind when it comes to umbilical cord care:

1. Wipe the umbilical cord dry: After the birth, the umbilical cord will be cut and then a stump will be left behind. It is important to wipe this stump dry after bathing and diaper changes to avoid infections.

2. Let the stump fall off naturally: The umbilical stump will dry out and fall off naturally after a few weeks. It is important not to pull or tear the umbilical stump, as this can cause bleeding or infection.

3. Clean the area around the belly button: After the stump has fallen off, it is important to clean the area around the belly button with a mild soap and water to avoid infections.

4. Avoid diapers or clothes that are tight around the belly button: It is important to avoid diapers or clothes that are tight around the belly button to avoid irritation or infection.

5. Seek medical attention for signs of infection: If the area around the navel becomes red, swollen or persistent, it is important to seek medical attention.

6.2. The benefits of breastfeeding

Breastfeeding has many benefits for both the newborn and the mother. Here are some of the benefits of breastfeeding:

1. Nutrition: Breast milk is the best source of nutrition for the newborn and provides all the nutrients it needs to grow and develop.

2. Immune system: Breast milk contains antibodies that help the newborn fight diseases and infections.

3. Bond between mother and baby: Breastfeeding can strengthen the bond between mother and baby and provide a feeling of closeness and security.

4. Reduced risk of diseases: Breastfeeding can reduce the risk of certain diseases in both the newborn and the mother, such as infections, allergies and some forms of cancer.

5. Convenient and cost-effective: Breastfeeding is convenient and cost-effective compared to formula.

It can take time to learn the technique of breastfeeding and it is important to get support and advice from a lactation consultant or midwife. If you cannot or choose to breastfeed, you can use breast milk substitute.

6.3. Aftercare after childbirth

After giving birth, it is important to take care of yourself and give your body time to recover. Here are some things to keep in mind when it comes to postpartum care:

1. Rest: It is important to rest and take it easy after giving birth to give the body time to recover.

2. Take care of the vagina: Aftercare of the vagina is important to avoid infections. Use cold compresses or warm baths to relieve pain and swelling.

3. Avoid heavy lifting: Avoid heavy lifting and strenuous activities during the first few weeks after delivery.

4. Eat healthy: After giving birth, it is important to eat healthy and get enough nutrients to give your body energy and strength.

5. Sleep: Sleep is important for recovery and caring for a newborn can make it difficult to get enough sleep. Try to rest when the baby sleeps and ask for help from a partner or family member to make time for rest and sleep.

6.4. Aftercare of the newborn

Aftercare of the newborn is also important to ensure that the little one has a good start in life. Here are some things to keep in mind when it comes to aftercare for the newborn:

1. Check weight: Regularly check the weight of the newborn to make sure he is getting enough nutrition and growing as he should.

2. Change diapers often: Change diapers often to avoid skin irritation and infections.

3. Keep the newborn warm: Make sure the newborn is kept warm by dressing him in layers of clothes or wrapping him in a blanket.

4. Sleep: Newborns sleep a lot and it is important that they get enough sleep to grow and develop. Try to have a regular sleep routine for the newborn.

5. Ask for help: Ask for help from family and friends to facilitate early care of the newborn. It is also important to seek medical help if there are any worrying signs or symptoms of illness in the newborn.

6.5. Recovery after caesarean section

If a cesarean delivery is needed, recovery may be different than after a vaginal delivery. Here are some things to keep in mind when it comes to recovering from a C-section:

1. Pain relief: The pain after a caesarean section can be severe and it is important to take pain medication as prescribed by the doctor.

2. Physical activity: After a cesarean delivery, the body needs time to heal. Physical activity should be limited during the first weeks after surgery.

3. Abdominal care: Abdominal care after a cesarean delivery is also important to avoid infections. Keep the wound clean and dry and follow the instructions of the doctor.

4. Support: After a cesarean birth, it can be difficult to care for a newborn. Ask for help from a partner, friends or family members.

5. Aftercare: It is also important to go to follow-up visits with the doctor to ensure that the wound is healing properly and to take care of any problems or complications.

6.6. Breastfeeding

Breastfeeding is a natural process that can take some time to learn. Here are some things to keep in mind when it comes to breastfeeding:

1. Positioning: Correct positioning is important to avoid pain and to ensure that the baby is getting enough milk.

2. Timing: Breastfeed as often as possible to provide the baby with sufficient nutrition and to stimulate milk production.

3. Behaviour: Watch the baby's behavior and try to breastfeed before he gets too hungry or too tired.

4. Support: Seek help from a lactation consultant or an experienced breastfeeding mother for support and advice.

5. Skin-to-skin contact: Skin-to-skin contact during breastfeeding can promote bonding between mother and baby.

6.7. Mental Health

After giving birth, it can be common to experience a range of emotions, including fatigue, overwhelming responsibility and anxiety. Here are some tips for taking care of your mental health after giving birth:

1. Sleep: Try to get enough sleep to avoid fatigue and exhaustion.

2. Support: Ask for help and support from partners, friends and family members.

3. Prioritization: Prioritize your own health and well-being.

4. Talk to someone: Talk to a doctor, psychologist or other professional if you feel overwhelmed or need more support.

5. Exercise: Regular exercise can help reduce stress and improve your mental health.

6. Activities: Continue to do activities that bring you joy and satisfaction.

7. Self-care: Take care of yourself by doing things that make you feel good, such as reading a book or taking a bath.

8. Medication: If you have a history of mental health problems, you may need medication after giving birth. Talk to your doctor about which options are best for you.

6.8. Return to sex life

Returning to sex can be a challenge after giving birth. Here are some things to consider:

1. Wait until you feel ready: It is important to wait until you feel ready both physically and mentally.

2. Communication: Talk to your partner about your needs and expectations.

3. Contraceptives: Talk to your doctor about which contraceptive methods are suitable for you.

4. Lubrication: Use lubrication if you need it to reduce pain and discomfort.

5. Take it easy: Take it easy and be careful the first few times.

6.9. Aftercare

After childbirth, it is important to get the right aftercare. Here are some things to consider:

1. Follow-up: Follow up with your doctor and/or midwife to ensure that you and your baby are healthy and that you are recovering properly.

2. Healthy lifestyle: Continue to eat a healthy diet and get regular exercise to help with recovery.

3. Support: Ask for help and support from partners, friends and family members.

4. Mental Health: Take care of your mental health by talking to someone and seeking help when needed.

5. Self-care: Take care of yourself by doing things that make you feel good.

6. Breastfeeding: Continue breastfeeding if possible to promote both your and your baby's health.

7. Contraceptives: Talk to your doctor about which contraceptives are suitable for you if you do not want to get pregnant again immediately after giving birth.

6.10. Summary

During pregnancy, the fetus undergoes an amazing journey from a simple cell to a fully developed human being. By understanding what happens each week, expectant parents can better prepare to take care of their health and their unborn child.

It is also important to remember that pregnancy can be challenging both physically and mentally, and that it is important to seek support and help when needed. By taking care of themselves and their unborn child, expectant parents can create a healthy and happy start to their new life as a family.

Final words

Dear reader,

We have now made it through an amazing journey that began with a miracle: when the sperm and the egg meet to form a zygote. From that moment on, the fetus has developed week by week, undergoing a series of fascinating changes that have enabled it to grow and mature inside the womb.

We have explored how the fetus develops from a simple cell into a fully developed human being, with all the organs, systems and abilities needed to survive and thrive in the outside world. We have seen how the fetus develops its brain and body, how its movements become increasingly coordinated, and how its senses and abilities grow and mature.

We have also discussed the challenges expectant parents may face during pregnancy and how they can best take care of themselves and their unborn children. From diet and exercise to aftercare and birth planning, we've covered a variety of topics relevant to all parents-to-be.

As we have seen, pregnancy is a time of great change and adaptation, both for the fetus and for the expectant parents. It is a time to appreciate the miraculous of what happens inside the womb and to prepare for the new phase of life as a family.

We hope that this book has been a helpful and informative guide for all expectant parents who want to learn more about their pregnancy and fetal development. Thank you for taking the time to join us on this amazing journey and we wish you all the happiness and health during your pregnancy and birth.

Made in the USA
Coppell, TX
22 November 2024

40771481R00072